Chrysalis

Poems of Motherhood's Light and Shadow

Dr Jigyansa Ipsita

BookLeaf Publishing

India | USA | UK

Made with ❤ on the BookLeaf Publishing Platform
www.bookleafpub.in
www.bookleafpub.com

Dedication

For all the women who have walked the complex path of motherhood— those who smiled when expected to cry, those who cried when expected to smile, those who felt everything at once, and those who felt nothing at all.

For the mothers who have questioned themselves, who have battled darkness while creating light, who have harbored fear alongside love, who have felt both trapped and transformed.

For the clinicians who listen without judgment, who recognize that growing a child and growing a mother are equally profound transformations.

For my own mother, who taught me that embracing the maternal journey is the greatest gift we can offer to those who come after us.

For my late father, whose wisdom still guides me, whose voice I hear in moments of doubt, who always believed in me and taught me that vulnerability is not weakness but courage in its purest form.

For both my brothers, Jingle and Kamal who provided

laughter when tears seemed more likely, who reminded
me of who I've always been even as I was becoming who
I needed to be.

For my sister-in-law, Lopa, who walked beside me with
understanding beyond experience, who offered wisdom
without presumption, who held space for both my joy
and sorrow.

For my husband, Sandeep, whose steady presence
anchored me through turbulent waters, whose love
never wavered even when I became someone new.

And for my little angel baby, Ekakshara, who made me
both stronger and more vulnerable than I ever thought
possible— you were worth every storm we weathered
together.

Preface

There is no manual for how a woman's mind navigates the landscape of pregnancy. Medical textbooks chart the physical transformation in clinical detail—the expanding uterus, the hormone surges, the developmental milestones of the growing fetus. But the parallel journey of the maternal psyche often remains unmapped, discussed in whispers if at all.

As both a psychiatrist and a mother, I have walked these territories from multiple perspectives. I have sat across from women struggling to articulate the complex emotional terrain of pregnancy, and I have lain awake at night, my own mind wrestling with the profound psychological shifts that come with creating life. These dual experiences revealed to me a troubling gap between how we prepare women for childbirth and how little we prepare them for the mental transformation that accompanies it.

This collection of poems attempts to illuminate the shadows—to give voice to the full spectrum of maternal mental experience, from the exquisite joy to the devastating darkness, from the mundane anxieties to the profound reckonings with identity and existence. Each poem represents a station on this journey, a moment of recognition for experiences often left unspoken.

Pregnancy is not merely a physical state but a psychological rite of passage. For some women, it unfolds as a relatively straightforward transition. For others, it becomes a battlefield where past traumas resurface, where mental health conditions intensify, where the fundamental sense of self undergoes radical reorganization. The poems in this collection honor both experiences and all that lie between.

My hope is that these words might serve as companions to those traversing their own maternal journeys—that in these pages, a woman might find her confusion, her fear, her grief, or her wonder reflected back to her with understanding. May she know she is neither alone nor abnormal in whatever she feels. May clinicians find in these verses a reminder of the profound inner work their pregnant patients undertake alongside the physical demands of childbearing.

And perhaps most importantly, may these poems contribute to a more honest cultural conversation about maternal mental health—one that acknowledges both the light and shadow of bringing life into the world, that recognizes the courage it takes to speak uncomfortable truths, and that extends compassion to all who undertake this ancient, ordinary, extraordinary transformation.

For in telling these stories, we begin to heal the silences that have isolated generations of mothers. In naming these experiences, we claim them as valid parts of the human journey. And in sharing these truths, we create space for a more nuanced, more honest understanding of what it means to become a mother—body, mind, and soul.

Acknowledgements

This collection would not exist without the courage of countless women who shared their pregnancy journeys with me—both as patients in my psychiatric practice and as friends who trusted me with their unfiltered truths. Their willingness to speak of the unspeakable, to name the shadows alongside the light, provided the foundation for these poems. While confidentiality prevents me from naming them individually, I hope they recognize their profound influence on these pages.

My deepest gratitude to my medical colleagues who understand that maternal mental health deserves the same attention and care as physical health. To the obstetricians, midwives, doulas, nurses, and fellow psychiatrists who have partnered with me in providing comprehensive care to pregnant and postpartum women: your dedication inspires me daily.

I am indebted to the researchers and advocates who have worked tirelessly to bring maternal mental health out of the shadows. Your studies, your policy work, your public education efforts have created the space for collections like this one to exist.

To the editor, whose belief in the importance of these poems never wavered, even when publishers questioned whether women would want to read about the darker aspects of pregnancy: your advocacy made this book possible.

My profound appreciation to my teachers, who encouraged me to find the balance between professional distance and human connection, who showed me how to carry others' pain without drowning in it, and who supported my dual path as both clinician and writer.

To the mothers in my own family, whose stories—both spoken and unspoken—formed my earliest understanding of maternal experience: thank you for whatever truths you were able to share, and for the silence that told me there was more to discover.

Finally, to my family, who lived alongside me through the writing of this collection: your patience with the late nights, the emotional aftermath of difficult poems, the times when I was present in body but absent in mind—all of this made this book possible. Your love is the safe harbor from which I could venture into these sometimes turbulent waters.

1. The Two Lines

In morning light, I stand alone, Holding fate in trembling hands— Two pink lines emerge like ancient runes, Drawing maps across my plans.
Truth revealed in bathroom stillness, Simple marks that change it all. I am vessel becoming voyage, Harbor answering the call.
Some women bloom like spring beneath this sign, Others fold inward with their fear. I float between these twin reactions, In twilight space, both far and near.
My fingers trace invisible constellations Across my still-flat universe of flesh, Where stardust gathers in secret chambers, Beginning what I cannot yet express.
Two lines. Clear as sunrise, deep as oceans, Thin as paper, strong as stone. The mathematics of miracle— The me I've been, the us unknown.
Time fractures—past and future Collide in this trembling moment. I'm both ending and beginning, Crescent moon and fullest moon.
Two lines. Before the news becomes a crown, Before the words escape my lips, I hold this quiet revelation Like

water in my cupped fingertips.
I am root becoming flower, Question folding into answer,
Division multiplied into wholeness— The paradox of
transformation.
Two lines. So small a thing to bear such weight,
Calligraphy of consequence. The simplest sign of
profound change— Poetry written in hormones and
hope.

2. Morning's Unwelcome Guest

Dawn arrives with bitter greeting, A slow tide rising in my throat. The bathroom floor, my cold companion, As waves of nausea set me afloat.
"Morning" sickness—cruelly misnamed, A shadow trailing through the day. My body, once familiar fortress, Now harbors storms I cannot sway.
Between the heaving and the hoping, I try to smile when others see. "It means it's healthy," they remind me, Small comfort when you cannot be.
The conference room spins slightly sideways, As I pretend that all is well. My colleague speaks of quarterly targets, While I map exits I know well.
This secret battle fought in silence, Behind closed doors and practiced smiles. My strength depleted by the hour, As simple tasks stretch into miles.
The scent of coffee—once beloved— Now turns my fragile world to ash. My emotions frayed like loosened stitches, As hormones surge and spirits crash.
How strange to nurture through rejection, To create

while being undone. This contradiction lives inside me—
Two heartbeats laboring as one.
At night I whisper to the darkness, "This sacrifice means
you will thrive." Then wake again to porcelain altars,
Where doubt and courage both arrive.
My mind and body now divided, One grateful, one in
mild revolt. The price of passage into motherhood— A
daily reckoning, exalt.
This guest that no one sees or welcomes, That drains the
color from my face, Becomes the measure of endurance—
The first test of maternal grace.

3. Ancestral Echoes

I trace the branches of my family tree, Where shadows hang like Spanish moss— Great-grandmother's "melancholy spells," Uncle's "nervous disposition," Mother's "low days" that stretched to months.
These whispered phrases, softened diagnoses, Dance in my blood alongside you.
At night, I dream of double helixes, Spiraling questions without answers: Will you inherit more than just my eyes? My anxious heart, my racing thoughts, The darkness that sometimes swallows light?
The therapist asks about my history, And I recite the litany of ghosts— Depression, anxiety, the cousin who Couldn't leave her house for years. The doctors nod and make their notes.
I feel you flutter, tiny dancer, As I check boxes on medical forms. "Family history of mental illness?" My pen hovers, then marks "Yes." Such weight in such a small gesture.
My mother calls to ask how I am feeling. I hear concern beneath her cheerfulness, The unspoken worry that I

might become What she became after I was born— A
woman drowning on dry land.
I place protective hands upon my belly, As if I could
shield you from invisible genes, From chemical
messengers and misfiring neurons, From the heritage we
never chose.
Yet in these same ancestral lines Run rivers of resilience,
Mountains of courage, Forests of fierce, protective love.
I vow to name the shadows for you, To light lanterns
where darkness gathers, To break the chains of silence
That made our family ghosts so powerful.
You kick against my ribs, And I imagine you declaring: "I
will write my own story."
And so will I, little one. So will I.

4. The Hormone Symphony

My body conducts an orchestra I never learned to play—
estrogen swelling like violins, progesterone's steady
drumbeat, cortisol's unexpected cymbals.
One moment, joy rises like a flute solo, clear and bright
and lifting. The next, a cello's mournful cry draws tears
for no reason at all.
Yesterday, I wept at a commercial for paper towels—a
family cleaning together, suddenly unbearably beautiful.
Today, I snapped at my partner for breathing too loudly,
rage erupting like brass horns.
The endocrinologist explains with clinical precision:
"Your hormones will increase by three hundred percent."
Numbers and charts that fail to capture this wild internal
weather, this tempest in previously calm waters.
My mother warned me about pregnancy emotions, but
not how foreign I would feel inside my skin, how quickly
the ground shifts beneath me, stability replaced by
chemical tides.
I wake in night sweats, sheets tangled around restless
legs, mind racing with vivid dreams and nameless

anxieties, the percussion of my heart too loud to allow
sleep.
Friends laugh knowingly about "pregnancy brain," as I
search for words that once came easily, as I forget
appointments and lose keys, my sharp mind now soft-
edged and wandering.
My doctor assures me this is normal, these mood swings
and memory gaps, this emotional hypersensitivity— the
price of growing another nervous system.
But normalcy offers little comfort when I no longer
recognize myself, when feelings wash through me like
waves, powerful enough to pull me under.
I try to separate what's "me" from what's "hormonal," but
the lines blur and dissolve. Am I still myself if everything
has changed? Is this new emotional landscape temporary
or transformation?
In quiet moments between crescendos, I place my hands
on my swelling abdomen, feeling the flutter of tiny
limbs, and understand—this chaos creates life.
The symphony plays on without my direction, ancient
and wise beyond my understanding, turning my body
into an instrument for the oldest music in the world.

5. Identity Divided

I stand before the mirror, half-recognizing the woman
who gazes back— her body softening in unfamiliar
places, her face fuller, eyes different somehow.
I try on my old self like a favorite sweater that no longer
quite fits. Career woman, independent spirit,
spontaneous friend, passionate lover— roles now
reshaping around this new center of gravity.
"You're still you," they reassure me, not understanding
that "me" is a moving target, a self dividing like cells
within me, becoming something simultaneously more
and less.
In meetings, I feel colleagues watching my expanding
form, their perception of me shifting before my
competence does. I speak about quarterly projections
while they see only approaching motherhood, as if my
mind has already departed on maternity leave.
At night, I dream of previous versions of myself walking
ahead on paths I can no longer follow, turning corners I
cannot see beyond, waving goodbye with a mixture of
sadness and relief.

My partner touches my changing body with wonder,
celebrating what I sometimes mourn in secret— the loss
of a shape I had finally learned to accept, a vehicle I had
finally learned to drive with confidence.
I sort through clothes I can no longer wear, each garment
a small funeral for former freedoms— the spontaneous
weekend trips, the late nights without consequence, the
body that belonged only to me.
Friends with children speak of motherhood as if it were a
destination I will soon reach, not understanding that I'm
already halfway there, inhabiting a liminal space with no
maps.
"Mother" feels like a borrowed costume I'm not yet
qualified to wear, while "myself" slips through my
fingers daily, leaving me grasping at a fading reflection.
No one warns you about this psychological splitting—
this cellular division of identity, this birthing of a new
self that must occur before the child arrives.
I practice saying "we" instead of "I," my vocabulary
evolving to accommodate this strange partnership of
bodies, this blurred boundary between beings.
In quiet moments, I whisper reassurances to both of us—
the woman I was, the mother I will be— promising
neither will completely disappear, that something
essential remains continuous.
This divided state is temporary and eternal, a bridge I'm

building as I cross it, the necessary transformation that
turns one life into two.

6. Body Estranged

My reflection has become a stranger— curves where
lines once were, swelling where flatness ruled, this body
morphing daily into territory uncharted.
I trace stretch marks like rivers across the expanding
landscape of my abdomen, silver-purple tributaries
marking the path of this necessary transformation.
Before pregnancy, I had achieved an uneasy truce with
my physical form— years of critical voices finally quieted
through hard-won battles for acceptance.
Now the rules of engagement change daily. The scale's
climbing numbers trigger old panic I thought I'd
overcome, old mantras of control rising unbidden.
"Your body is doing exactly what it should," my doctor
says with clinical approval, not seeing how each gained
pound resurrects ghosts I had finally laid to rest.
At night, my partner's hands hesitate over this changing
topography, and I wonder if his pause mirrors my own
uncertainty— this body both miraculous and
unrecognizable.
In prenatal yoga, the instructor celebrates our ripe,

fertile forms with reverent words, while I struggle to
breathe through the discomfort of taking up space I was
taught to minimize.
I avoid the fitness influencers, their post-baby bounce-
back photos, their promises of reclaiming what is "lost,"
as if this journey allows for return tickets.
For those of us who fought for peace with the bodies we
inhabited before, pregnancy arrives as both blessing and
ambush— necessary surrender after hard-won control.
I stand naked before the mirror, trying to see this form
through different eyes— not as beauty gained or lost but
as function perfected, purpose embodied.
Some days I succeed. Some days the old voices win.
Some days I exist between appreciation and alienation,
between marvel and mourning.
I place hands on the taut drum of my belly, feeling the
flutter-kicks of the reason for all this magnificent
disruption, this biological revolution.
And in that moment of connection, body and purpose
align briefly in perfect clarity— this temporary
estrangement a necessary price for miraculous
harboring.

7. Insomnia's Cradle

Night stretches endless before me, a desert of hours I
must cross alone while the world around me slumbers,
oblivious to my wide-eyed vigilance.
Sleep—once a reliable friend— has become a fickle
visitor, appearing briefly before vanishing, leaving me
stranded in consciousness.
I shift my unwieldy body, pillow between knees, under
belly, behind back, a fortress of fabric that fails to deliver
comfort.
The digital clock glows accusingly: 2:17, 3:42, 4:05— each
number a small defeat, each hour a test of endurance.
My mind races in the darkness, planning nurseries and
worrying over names, calculating finances and delivery
dates, a midnight marathon of thoughts.
Just as exhaustion finally pulls me under, a tiny foot
lodges firmly against my ribs, a hiccup ripples through
my abdomen— my child already keeping me awake.
The cruelest irony: bone-deep fatigue paired with
stubborn wakefulness, as if my body is rehearsing for the
sleepless months to come.

Morning arrives with hollow eyes and a fog that follows
me through the day, dulling my thoughts, slurring my
words, making simple tasks seem monumental.
"Sleep while you can," well-meaning voices advise, not
understanding that I would if I could, that this insomnia
is not choice but condition, not preparation but preview.
The experts offer their suggestions: lavender oil, white
noise, warm milk, relaxation techniques and bedtime
routines— small weapons against a powerful foe.
My doctor explains the physiology: hormones,
discomfort, frequent urination, restless legs and racing
hearts— as if naming the thieves will return what's
stolen.
I read that chronic sleep deprivation can mimic
depression's symptoms, can trigger anxiety's sharp
edges, can blur the line between coping and crisis.
In daylight, I function through the fog, in meetings,
nodding to hide my exhaustion, smiling through yawns
that crack my jaw, pretending alertness I do not feel.
At night, I lie beside my sleeping partner, watching the
ceiling, counting breaths, wondering if this is
preparation or punishment, this lesson in sustained
wakefulness.
Dawn breaks, and I greet it with red eyes, another night
crossed off the calendar, another day to endure half-
present, rocking in insomnia's relentless cradle.

8. Hypervigilance

Each twinge becomes a question mark, each pain a
potential warning— is this normal, is this dangerous, is
this the beginning of an ending?
I count kicks like rosary beads, ten movements before I
can exhale, marking time between flutters, clock
watching with mounting anxiety.
My phone holds a dozen pregnancy apps, each one
consulted for reassurance that this sensation or that
symptom falls within the bounds of ordinary.
The doctor's number saved as favorite, thumb hovering
over the call button whenever silence stretches too long
in my carefully monitored womb.
I analyze the color of everything— discharge, urine, the
veins beneath my skin— searching for signs of trouble in
the body I no longer fully trust.
At night, I wake to place my hand on my swollen
abdomen, holding still until I feel that reassuring nudge,
that proof of continued existence.
The list of forbidden things grows daily— foods,
activities, positions, thoughts— as I construct elaborate

defenses against invisible threats to this fragile life.
Friends notice my constant alertness, the way my hand
reflexively finds my belly, how conversation stops mid-
sentence when I feel something new or nothing at all.
The statistics both comfort and terrify— ninety-eight
percent chance of normalcy still leaves two percent
possibility of loss, odds I calculate with obsessive
precision.
Medical terminology becomes my second language—
preeclampsia, placenta previa, gestational diabetes—
words I never wanted to know now familiar as my own
heartbeat.
Is this instinct or illness? Protection or paranoia? The
line between maternal concern and anxiety's sharp edge
grows thin.
The sonographer notes my quickened breath, the tension
in my jaw as the wand moves across my gel-slicked skin,
seeking the whoosh-whoosh that means safety.
"Try to relax," they tell me, not understanding that
vigilance has become my full-time occupation, my
contribution to this child's survival.
Every pregnancy book warns of stress, of anxiety's
impact on developing brains, creating a recursive loop of
worry about worry, fear about the effects of fear itself.
Yet in the midnight hours, when doubts crowd loudest in
my mind, I recognize this hypervigilance as love's first
anxious language.

9. The Waiting Room

Sterile chairs arranged in hopeful rows, magazines no
one really reads, soft voices calling names that aren't
mine, not yet.
The clock on the wall moves glacially, each minute an
exercise in patience as we wait for science to peer inside,
to measure, to predict, to know.
Around me sit other women, some with rounded bellies
evident, others with secrets still concealed, all of us
suspended in anticipation.
The forms I've filled ask for family histories— genetic
conditions, inherited diseases, chromosomal anomalies—
a catalog of potential disasters.
I've checked boxes and circled numbers, translated my
lineage into risk factors, wondering which ancestral gifts
might become burdens for you.
My name is finally called. The technician's face reveals
nothing as cold gel spreads across my skin, as the wand
searches for revelations.
The screen shows shadowy geography, a universe
forming within me, while I scan the technician's eyes for

reassurance she cannot ethically give.
"The doctor will discuss the results," she says, her
neutrality a wall I cannot scale with anxious questions,
with pleas for immediate certainty.
And so begins another waiting— hours or days of
imagined outcomes, of statistics and probabilities, of
hope battling against fear.
My phone remains too close at hand, checked too
frequently for missed calls, for the news that will pivot
my world toward relief or toward grief.
Some tests promise knowledge of gender, as if knowing
"boy" or "girl" might soften the sharper question:
"healthy" or "challenged" or "compatible with life."
I rehearse acceptance of every scenario, trying on
possible futures like clothes, wondering which I will
eventually wear, which will become my life's new skin.
Other mothers share waiting room wisdom— stories of
false positives and needless worry, of dire predictions
proven wrong, of surprising strength found in difficulty.
The genetic counselor speaks of odds, of bell curves and
standard deviations, reducing my child to percentages
that both comfort and terrify.
In this liminal space between knowing and not, I am
learning pregnancy's hardest lesson: that certainty is
luxury, not right, that parenthood begins with surrender.
The phone finally rings. I answer with heart suspended,

breath held like a prayer, ready to receive whatever comes next.

10. Prenatal Depression's Mask

I smile when they ask how I'm feeling, the practiced
curve of lips that never reaches my eyes. "Glowing," I
say, because that's what they expect, what the magazines
promise, what the myth demands.
Behind this mask, a wasteland stretches— barren, gray,
impenetrable— my emotions flattened to a single, endless
plain where joy should bloom but cannot take root.
"It's the happiest time of your life," they say with such
conviction that I nod in false agreement, ashamed to
confess the emptiness within.
Each prenatal visit, a questionnaire: "In the past two
weeks, have you felt down, depressed, or hopeless?" My
pen hovers over "rarely" though "constantly" is true, fear
of judgment guiding my dishonesty.
This child was wanted, planned for, dreamed of— how
then to explain the disconnect, the absence of maternal
bliss, the dread that fills the spaces joy should occupy?
I watch other pregnant women in the park, their hands
caressing swollen bellies with evident love, their faces

bright with anticipation, and wonder what broken piece inside me prevents such feeling.

Sleep offers no refuge— insomnia paired with nightmares when rest does come, dark visions of inadequacy and failure, of a child who senses my emotional absence.

The nursery stands half-finished, each abandoned project a testament to energy I cannot summon, to connection I cannot forge.

My partner watches me with worried eyes, careful questions met with careful lies, both of us tiptoeing around the growing darkness, neither naming the shadow in our home.

The obstetrician asks about physical symptoms— blood pressure, swelling, aches and pains— but rarely questions the state of my mind, as if the neck up exists separately from conception.

How to explain that I'm drowning in dry air? That breathing requires conscious effort? That the simplest tasks—showering, dressing, eating— have become mountains I lack the strength to climb?

I read that prenatal depression affects one in ten, that hormone shifts can trigger chemicals cascading, that history of depression heightens risk, that it's not my fault—yet shame persists.

One day, the mask slips. Tears come in my mother's kitchen, sudden and unstoppable, the dam of pretense finally breaking.

Her arms around me, permission granted: "I felt the same carrying you," she whispers, generations of hidden suffering suddenly visible in shared confession.
The words finally spoken aloud— "I think I need help"— the hardest admission becoming the first step toward light.
The psychiatrist explains treatment options, weighing risks against benefits, reminding me that my mental health creates the foundation for my child's.
Slowly, with therapy and careful support, medication considered with caution, community found in others' stories, the wasteland shows signs of thaw.
Depression doesn't end with a single confession, but naming it reduces its power, removes the exhaustion of disguise, allows space for genuine feeling—whatever form it takes.
The mask set aside, I learn to answer honestly when asked, to accept help when offered, to forgive myself for an illness never chosen.

11. Medicating for Two

The orange prescription bottle sits on my nightstand,
pills I've taken faithfully for years, my mind's necessary
equilibrium now a complicated ethical equation.
The psychiatrist lays out the options with careful,
measured words— benefits weighed against risks, my
stability against unknown impacts.
"Category C," he explains, clinical shorthand for "we
cannot be certain," for "animal studies show possible
effects," for "human data is insufficient."
I research obsessively at night, medical journals and
forum posts, seeking certainty where none exists,
desperate for the right answer to reveal itself.
Some women speak of stopping cold, of weathering the
withdrawal storm, of minds unraveling during
pregnancy for the sake of theoretical protection.
Others testify to medications continued, to healthy
babies born despite the fear, to the necessity of maternal
mental health as foundation for the child's wellbeing.
My obstetrician and psychiatrist confer, comparing notes
across specialties, this rare collaboration evidence of

how much hangs in the balance.

"What would you do?" I ask them both, seeking guidance beyond statistics, beyond the cold calculus of risk assessment, beyond the sterile language of informed consent.

They cannot tell me, cannot decide what trade-offs I should make, what potential outcomes I can live with, what gambles I am willing to take.

I think of airplane safety briefings— secure your own mask before assisting others— wondering if the same wisdom applies to the oxygen of mental stability.

Each night I hold a pill in my palm, this tiny chemical constellation that keeps my darkness at bay, that allows me to function, to thrive.

I think of the brain forming inside me, delicate neural pathways developing, synapses connecting and disconnecting, vulnerability beyond my comprehension.

Friends offer unsolicited opinions: "Better safe than sorry," some insist, "You need to be well," others counter, each perspective clouding my clarity.

I recall my last episode— the bottomless well of despair, the thoughts of ending it all, the hospitalization that finally helped.

Could I survive that again while pregnant? Could a child survive my unmedicated mind? What damage might untreated illness cause compared to medication's uncertain effects?

I make my decision day by day, pill by pill, heartbeat by heartbeat, trusting the careful calibration of dosage adjusted for dual consideration.

The guilt remains a constant companion, second-guessing with each swallow, fear flaring with each prenatal test, "What if?" echoing through sleepless nights.

Yet in this impossible choice, I find a fierce maternal wisdom— the recognition that caring for myself is the first act of caring for you.

I whisper promises as I take each dose, hand resting on my growing abdomen: "I'm doing my best with impossible choices. I'm choosing us both, as best I can."

12. Past Trauma's Echo

The paper gown crinkles as I shift, feet in cold stirrups,
body exposed, the familiar vulnerability rushing back
like floodwaters breaking through a dam.
"Just relax," the doctor says, not seeing how those words
trigger memories of other voices, other hands, other
times I was told to surrender control.
My breath catches, vision narrows, the examination
room dissolving into another place, another time, trauma
folding years like origami.
The nurse notices my white knuckles, the trembling I
cannot contain, and asks with unexpected gentleness,
"Would you like someone to hold your hand?"
On intake forms, there was no box to check for "my body
remembers violation," for "medical exams trigger
flashbacks," for "pregnancy makes me feel colonized
again."
My therapist taught me grounding techniques— five
things I can see, four I can touch, three I can hear, two I
can smell, one I can taste—present over past.
I try to focus: ceiling tiles, stirrups, blood pressure cuff,

paper sheet, the clock's tick, voices in the hall, antiseptic scent, my own metallic fear.

Pregnancy requires such surrender of privacy— body prodded, measured, assessed, strangers granted access to intimate spaces, medical necessity overriding personal boundaries.

For those of us carrying histories of assault, each examination becomes a battlefield where past and present collide, where healing meets fresh wounding.

I didn't know how childbearing would resurrect what I thought was safely buried— the violation now echoed in medical necessity, power dynamics replicated in sterile rooms.

My partner waits outside, unaware of the war waging behind these doors, how I fight to stay present for our child while the past pulls me under.

Some providers understand without explanation— they ask permission before touching, narrate each action before it occurs, respect the "no" I sometimes need to voice.

Others brush aside hints of discomfort, focused on medical protocol, unaware how their well-meaning efficiency triggers ancient survival responses.

I find allies in unexpected places— a nurse who notices my dissociation, a midwife who offers alternative positions, a doula who stands guard over my dignity.

I learn to advocate with shaking voice: "I have a history

of trauma." "I need you to explain before you touch." "I might need to pause during procedures."
Some days are easier than others. Some appointments leave me intact. Others require hours of aftercare, of gentle reassembly of fragmented self.
Pregnancy books never mention how growing life inside a previously violated body creates complex layers of reclamation, of triumph intertwined with terror.
Yet in this journey through haunted landscape, I am learning to hold contradictions: that my body can be both battlefield and sanctuary, that past wounds and new life can coexist.
Each prenatal visit survived, each trigger weathered without drowning, becomes its own victory, its own healing— not just for me, but for the child who grows.
For I am breaking cycles with each breath, rewriting stories with each boundary upheld, creating safety from the ashes of violation, turning trauma's echo into freedom's song.

13. Partnership Realigned

We lie in bed, your hand on my growing belly, a gesture once intimate, now shared with a third, our private language of touch evolving into something neither of us yet fully understands.

"I feel like I'm losing you," you confess in darkness, words falling into the space between our bodies, a space growing literally and figuratively as this pregnancy reshapes more than just my form.

We were once perfect counterweights, balanced in our give and take, now tipping toward unfamiliar asymmetry — my body's demands creating new inequalities.

You bring me ginger tea for nausea, massage cramping legs with gentle hands, attend appointments with attentive ears, yet feel sidelined in this biological revolution.

I seek comfort in your embrace, only to pull away without explanation, hormones rendering your familiar scent suddenly intolerable, mysteriously repellent.

Our intimacy transforms— sexual desire ebbs and flows unpredictably, sometimes flooding, sometimes vanishing,

my body's priorities mysteriously reordered.
The baby kicks, and I grab your hand, placing it where
tiny feet press outward, this shared moment of wonder
bridging briefly the separate experiences of carrying and
witnessing.
We argue about names, nursery colors, parenting
philosophies still theoretical, these surface
disagreements masking deeper fears: Will we survive
this fundamental transformation?
Friends warn us with knowing smiles: "Sleep now while
you can," "Remember each other when baby comes," as if
we might forget what built this love.
You find me crying over laundry, something so small
becoming insurmountable, and the look of helpless
concern in your eyes mirrors my own confusion at these
tidal emotions.
At birthing class, we practice breathing, your steady
counts guiding my inhalations, rehearsing for labor's
intensity, learning new ways to navigate pain together.
The books all talk of motherhood, fewer speak of
partnerships weathering change, of relationships
stretched and reconfigured, of love expanded but also
tested.
When anxiety grips me at midnight, fears of inadequacy
stealing sleep, you listen without offering solutions,
learning that presence matters more than answers.
Your hand on the small of my back, steadying me as my

center of gravity shifts, becomes metaphor for what
we're learning: support without control, presence
without demand.
Some evenings we sit in comfortable silence, your head
against my shoulder, hand on my belly, three heartbeats
finding their rhythm, family forming in the quiet
between words.
We are learning a new choreography, stepping on toes,
missing cues, starting over, clumsy in this dance we've
never practiced, yet somehow moving forward together.
"We're still us," I whisper in the dark, "just becoming
more than we were before," your fingers intertwining
with mine, partnership realigning around this growing
miracle.

14. Work and Womb

I sit in the conference room, suit jacket unbuttoned over
my growing belly, nodding at quarterly projections while
counting fetal movements beneath the table.
My colleagues' eyes flicker to my abdomen during my
presentation on market strategy, their perceptions
shifting visibly from professional to pregnant— as if the
two states cannot coexist.
"When are you due?" replaces "What do you think of the
proposal?" My expertise suddenly secondary to my
reproductive status.
I find myself speaking louder in meetings, asserting
competence with extra vigor, fighting the subtle erosion
of credibility that comes with visible motherhood.
The women's restroom becomes sanctuary for quiet
moments of nausea, for silent tears of fatigue, for
adjusting waistbands and expectations.
My supervisor asks about my "plans" with careful
corporate neutrality, the unspoken question hanging:
Will you be one who returns or doesn't?
I calculate sick days against prenatal appointments,

measure bladder urgency against meeting lengths, time snacks for blood sugar stability between client calls and presentations.

The pregnancy books never mention how to respond when a client says, "Should you be working in your condition?" or how to handle water breaking in the office.

My out-of-office reply is drafted months early, contingency plans created for projects, handover notes prepared meticulously, motherhood approached with professional thoroughness.

Other mothers in the workplace offer knowing glances, subtle assistance, warnings about the pumping room's inadequacy, advice on navigating the invisible maternal penalty.

The career ladder I've climbed steadily suddenly seems to have missing rungs, opportunities subtly redirected away from my "divided attention."

I overhear conversations about "commitment" when colleagues think I cannot hear, as if growing life diminishes ambition, as if motherhood and achievement are opposing forces.

In bathroom mirrors, I practice responses to intrusive questions about "coming back," to assumptions about my professional future, to the subtle devaluation of my working self.

The emails arrive at midnight, when insomnia keeps me

awake, and I answer them with one hand, the other
pressed against kicking feet.
Each day becomes a balance of creation— presentations
and human development, client relationships and
maternal bonds, professional identity and emerging
parenthood.
I research maternity leave policies with the same
diligence I apply to market analysis, finding the gaps and
inconsistencies, the ways systems still fail to
accommodate creation.
Yet in this clash of worlds, this integration of working
and growing, I am pioneering my own path forward,
refusing to diminish either aspect of myself.
For in this dual productivity, this simultaneous building
of career and family, lies a revolutionary act of
wholeness— bringing my complete self to both worlds I
inhabit.

15. The Nesting Compulsion

Three a.m. finds me organizing baby clothes by size, color, season, practicality— tiny garments arranged with precision that would make military sergeants proud. Yesterday I cleaned baseboards with a toothbrush, today I've alphabetized the spice rack, tomorrow I'll sort the linen closet for the third time this week.
"Nesting," they call it with indulgent smiles, this sudden, overwhelming urge to order chaos, to scrub and sort and sanitize, to prepare the world for precious cargo.
But beneath the normal maternal instinct lurks something more insistent, less controlled— thoughts that circle like restless birds, refusing to settle despite exhaustion.
What begins as practical preparation slides imperceptibly into compulsion— checking and rechecking locked doors, counting and recounting newborn socks.
I arrange stuffed animals by height, then rearrange them by softness, then organize them by color spectrum, unable to stop until it feels "just right."

My partner finds me tearful in the nursery, surrounded
by dismantled furniture, convinced the crib's slight tilt
might somehow harm our sleeping child.
"It's normal to worry," the books all say, but they don't
mention hands raw from washing, or the inability to
sleep until all bottles have been sterilized in perfect
order.
For some of us, pregnancy amplifies tendencies
previously managed or mild— the need for control
finding fertile ground in the fundamental
uncontrollability of birth.
OCD whispers its deceptive promises: "If everything is
perfect, nothing will go wrong." "If you check one more
time, you'll be safe." "If you worry enough, you prevent
disaster."
The doctor listens without judgment when I finally admit
the rituals, the intrusive thoughts of harm, the
exhausting mental vigilance.
"Pregnancy can trigger or worsen anxiety disorders," she
explains with compassionate clarity. "Hormones affect
neurotransmitters, and massive life changes test coping
mechanisms."
The line between normal nesting and pathological
perfectionism blurs in the vulnerable months when
protection feels like sacred duty.
I learn to recognize the difference: Healthy preparation
energizes and satisfies. Anxious compulsion depletes and

distresses. One builds a home; the other builds a prison. With gentle guidance, I develop new patterns— setting timers for cleaning sessions, asking for reality checks when doubt spirals, practicing tolerating small imperfections.

Some days are easier than others. Some triggers still send me straightening, ordering. But I'm learning to redirect the energy, to channel the protective instinct productively.

I fold onesies with deliberate mindfulness, allowing some to remain slightly wrinkled, whispering to myself and my growing child: "Good enough is perfect enough for us."

The nursery doesn't need hospital-grade sterility. The drawers don't require military precision. What my child will need most is a mother present, not perfect.

Still, I sort tiny socks into pairs, smooth blankets with careful hands, prepare this nest with loving attention— nourishing instinct without feeding obsession.

16. Ante-Partum

The darkness arrives without warning, settling over me
like heavy snowfall, muffling joy, dampening light, a
silent depression few discuss.
They speak often of postpartum shadows, of blues that
follow birth's intensity, but rarely of the darkness that
can come before, the despair that visits while still
carrying life.
"Shouldn't you be happy?" voices imply, confusion in
their well-meaning concern, as if pregnancy guarantees
emotional sunshine, as if growing life precludes growing
darkness.
I move through days like a sleepwalker, performing the
motions of preparation, attending appointments, taking
vitamins, while emptiness echoes within.
The prenatal forms ask about feeling down, little boxes
to check for mild symptoms, unprepared for the depth of
the abyss that swallows motivation, pleasure, hope.
Sleep either eludes me completely or claims me for
stretches too long, my body heavy with more than child,
weighted with inexplicable sorrow.

Food loses flavor, colors fade to gray, the world perceived
through thick glass, disconnected from my changing
body, from the life supposedly bringing purpose.
My doctor watches with careful eyes when I cannot meet
her gaze, when tears come during routine questions,
when responses lack appropriate animation.
"Antepartum depression," she finally names it, "affects up
to one in seven pregnancies, often overlooked, often
untreated, shadowed by the myth of maternal bliss."
The diagnosis brings relief of recognition, permission to
acknowledge suffering, to understand this is not
weakness or ingratitude, but legitimate illness requiring
care.
Darker thoughts sometimes surface, frightening in their
intensity— wondering if I or the baby would be better
unborn, if this mistake of motherhood might end.
These thoughts send me reaching for help, whispering
shameful confessions to professionals who respond not
with horror but with protocols designed for this very
crisis.
Treatment options are carefully weighed— therapy,
support networks, medication when needed, the risks of
untreated depression balanced against intervention's
uncertainties.
My partner learns to sit with my silence, to encourage
without demanding happiness, to witness suffering
without trying to fix, to believe in my return when I

cannot.

Some days, brief moments of connection come— a flutter of movement in my belly, a sudden awareness of life beyond my pain, small footholds on the climb back toward light.

Recovery comes not as sudden sunrise but as gradual lightening of darkness, moments of engagement lengthening slowly, capacity for hope expanding incrementally.

I learn to forgive myself for this struggle, to understand depression's appearance not as maternal failure but as medical reality, as valid in pregnancy as any other time. For those who walk this shadowed path, carrying life while fighting for our own, there is no shame in naming the darkness, in seeking light when most believe we already glow.

17. Birth Expectations

I collect birth stories like talismans, each narrative
searched for clues and omens, for warnings and
reassurances, for the map to safe passage.
In birth class, we practice positions, breathing
techniques, visualizations— rehearsing for a performance
with an unpredictable script.
My birth plan spans three detailed pages: preferences for
lighting and music, requests for minimal interventions,
contingencies carefully considered.
"The body knows what to do," they say, these mothers
with memories softened by time, these midwives with
professional confidence, these books with serene
birthing images.
Yet my nights fill with hospital nightmares— emergency
surgeries, blaring alarms, masked faces speaking in
urgent tones, pain beyond my capacity to endure.
The doula teaches partner hip squeezes, counterpressure
techniques, encouraging phrases, props and tools to ease
the journey, as if labor can be managed with proper
preparation.

I tour the birthing center, noting tubs and birthing balls,
ambient lighting and homey touches, trying to envision
myself in this transformative space.
But deep within, fear coils tightly— ancient, instinctual,
resistant to reason— the primal knowledge that this
threshold has claimed women throughout history.
Some friends share empowering stories: births described
as "intense but manageable," "the most powerful
experience of my life," "painful but purposeful, and
absolutely worth it."
Others whisper harsher truths: "I thought I would die
from the pain," "Nothing went according to plan," "I'm
still processing the trauma years later."
The gap between expectation and experience stretches
before me like an unbridgeable chasm, no amount of
preparation guaranteeing which narrative will become
mine.
My doctor discusses pain management options,
statistical risks and benefits of each choice, her clinical
detachment both comforting and concerning as she
outlines what might go wrong.
For those with previous trauma, childbirth looms as
potential retrigger, the loss of control, the physical
vulnerability echoing past violations in new context.
I practice surrendering small controls, tiny rehearsals for
the great relinquishment, for the moment when plans
must yield to the unstoppable force of nature.

"You are stronger than you think," my mother offers as
comfort, her own birth stories softened by decades,
selective memory a merciful gift.
Between breaths in meditation practice, I acknowledge
the contradictory truths: Birth is natural and birth is
dangerous. Birth is beautiful and birth is brutal.
The unknown awaits beyond these final weeks, my body
preparing for what my mind cannot— the ultimate
surrender, the painful passage, the transformation that
cannot be rehearsed.
All expectations will likely shatter against the reality of
my unique experience, yet I continue preparing,
planning, hoping, gathering courage for the journey
ahead.

18. NICU Vigil

The nursery at home sits perfect, waiting, while I keep
vigil by a plastic box where my child lies tethered to
machines, our beginning nothing like I'd dreamed.
Beeping monitors become my lullabies, oxygen
saturation my obsession, the rise and fall of tiny
bandaged chest the focus of my desperate attention.
Three pounds four ounces of fragile life, skin translucent,
veins a delicate map, each breath a victory, each gram
gained celebrated like mountainous achievement.
The nurses know my child better than I do— how she
tolerates feedings, which alarms mean emergency and
which mean adjustment, the intimate details of care I
should provide.
I learn a foreign language overnight: bradycardia, apnea,
gavage feeding, surfactant, bilirubin, desaturation—
clinical terms describing my heart's treasure.
My hands, once imagined cradling a swaddled newborn,
now reach through porthole openings, touching with
featherlight pressure, afraid of bruising paper-thin skin.
I pump milk on rigid schedule, liquid gold measured in

milliliters, each drop a connection between us, when
arms cannot offer their embrace.
The kangaroo care hour becomes sacred ritual— shirt
opened, tiny body placed against my chest, wires and
tubes carefully arranged to allow this brief illusion of
normalcy.
Other parents nod in hushed understanding across the
artificial landscape of the NICU, our community forged
in fluorescent light, united by fear, hope, and sterilization
protocols.
Days blur into nights, hospital corridors becoming more
familiar than my own home, time measured not in hours
but in medical rounds, in incremental progress or
frightening setbacks.
My partner and I pass like ships, tag-teaming presence at
the incubator, relaying medical updates instead of sweet
nothings, our relationship strained by shared terror.
I call for updates at midnight, 3 AM, dawn, nurses
patient with my repeated questions, my need for control
in this uncontrollable situation, my desperate search for
certainty where none exists.
I learn to celebrate tiny victories: first time breathing
unassisted for an hour, first full teaspoon fed without
residual, first time holding without bradycardia alarms.
The journey of motherhood transformed from expected
joy to unexpected endurance, from natural bonding to
technological intervention, from bringing baby home to

daily hospital commute.

Guilt arrives uninvited at odd hours— did my body fail to provide safe harbor? Could I have prevented this premature arrival? Am I less a mother for needing medical proxy?

Developmental specialists offer gentle counsel: "Your voice is medicine, your presence healing. Read, sing, touch when allowed. Be the constant in this clinical environment."

Other NICU graduates visit occasionally, toddlers and teens who began as tiny fighters, their parents offering the most precious gift: visual proof that this purgatory can end.

I keep midnight vigil by the warming bed, watching shadows shift across my child's face, whispering promises I'm unsure I can keep, prayers to deities I'm unsure I believe in.

One day, the doctor mentions "discharge planning," words that spark both terror and desperate hope, the finish line appearing on distant horizon, our marathon of waiting approaching transition.

We will carry this experience within us always, this birth by fire, this parenthood baptized in fear, this love forged in fluorescent light and antiseptic, stronger perhaps for having begun in struggle.

19. Postpartum Storm

They handed you to me, still slick with birth, tiny body
against my heaving chest, and waited for the rush of love
that everyone promised would come.
I felt... nothing. Emptiness where emotion should flood,
disconnection where bonding should bloom, a vast
hollow space where joy should reside.
The nurses speak of "baby blues," a tidy phrase for
temporary tears, a normal dip in hormonal seas— not
this drowning I cannot name.
Days pass in blur of feeding attempts, diaper changes,
sleepless nights, mechanical motions performed by
hands that seem disconnected from my will.
Visitors exclaim, "Isn't motherhood amazing?" And I nod,
smile, perform the expected role, while inside screaming:
"I feel nothing for this child. What kind of monster have
I become?"
My partner watches with growing concern, gentle
questions met with reassurances, both of us afraid to
speak aloud the darkness gathering in our home.
I stare at your sleeping face, searching for the fierce love

others describe, finding only duty, responsibility, the
weight of a life dependent on a shell.
Intrusive thoughts arrive unbidden— images of harm I
would never cause, fears that make me recoil from
myself, terror that someone will see the truth.
The questionnaire at my six-week checkup: "How often
have you felt down, depressed, hopeless?" My pen circles
"rarely" while my soul screams "constantly," shame
silencing my cry for intervention.
At night, I fantasize about disappearing, about a life
before your arrival, about sleep uninterrupted by cries,
about an identity not consumed by failure.
One morning, I cannot rise from bed, limbs heavy with
invisible weight, tears flowing without sound or end, the
facade finally crumbling completely.
My sister finds me curled and vacant, the baby wailing
unattended nearby, and makes the call I couldn't make
myself, speaking words I couldn't form: "She needs help
now."
The psychiatrist names the storm: "Postpartum
depression," she says with calm certainty. "One in seven
mothers," she continues, "Not weakness, not choice, not
failure—illness."
The diagnosis falls like prison doors opening, permission
to acknowledge suffering, to step out of shame's isolating
cell, to rejoin humanity as someone sick, not evil.
Treatment begins with gentle persistence— medication

to rebalance chemistry gone rogue, therapy to untangle thought from distortion, community to prove I'm not alone in this.

Recovery comes not as sudden sunshine but as gradual lifting of the heaviest clouds, moments of connection strung together, brief attachments lengthening into bonds.

The first time I feel it—a spark of warmth as you gaze at me with total trust, a flicker of protective instinct, the beginning of what might grow into love.

Each day, the storm recedes a little more, allowing space for something new to grow— not the instant passion others described, but a slower, hard-won attachment, no less real.

I learn that maternal love has many forms, that bonding follows different timelines, that postpartum mood disorders are medical events, not moral failings or maternal deficiencies.

For those who walk through similar storms, I leave breadcrumbs along the darkened path: There is shore beyond this raging sea. You are not alone. You are not to blame. Help exists. Light returns. Love comes, in time.

20. Nursing Grief

I prepared for the pain of childbirth, but not for this—the
rawness of cracked nipples, the fever of mastitis, the toe-
curling latch, the muffled sobs at 3 a.m. feedings.
"Breast is best," the posters proclaim in cheerful fonts
with smiling mothers, their babies effortlessly nursing, a
natural bond I cannot seem to forge.
The lactation consultant repositions my hold,
demonstrates the "sandwich technique" again, her
clinical touch on my exposed flesh adding humiliation to
frustration.
Each feeding becomes a battleground, your tiny face red
with hunger and rage, my body tensing with anticipated
pain, both of us crying through the struggle.
The pump whirs in mechanical rhythm, extracting
precious drops measured in milliliters, my worth as
mother seemingly calculated in ounces of milk produced
and consumed.
Well-meaning voices offer contradictory advice: "Try
harder." "Don't stress." "It's just supply." "Keep at it."
"Consider supplementing." Their words clustering like

stones in my stomach.

Formula cans sit in the back of the cupboard, emergency rations I view with complex shame, simultaneously salvation and admission of defeat, my insurance against your hunger.

My partner finds me weeping over a bottle, hard-won breast milk accidentally spilled, white liquid spreading across the counter like my maternal hopes dissolving before me.

The scale at the pediatrician tells its ruthless truth: not gaining enough, percentiles dropping, the doctor's concern barely masked as she suggests "supplementing for now."

I mourn what I imagined this would be— the natural nourishment, the bonding ritual, the empowered maternal body functioning as designed, the idealized image I cannot manifest.

My identity fractures along with my areolas, the good mother I strived to be versus the failing one I've become, inadequate at the most basic biological function.

The online groups polarize around methods, militant camps defending territory while I sit alone at night, searching for permission to prioritize mental health over milk supply.

What no one mentioned: sometimes bodies don't comply, sometimes babies don't coordinate suck and swallow, sometimes ancestral wisdom requires modern support,

sometimes feeding your child means finding another
way.
The first time I give you formula, watching you drink
with relieved vigor, I experience both sharp grief and
sudden liberation, the complex calculus of surrender.
Postpartum anxiety, already hovering, found fertile
ground in feeding failure, each tearful nursing session
reinforcing the insidious whisper: "Not good enough."
Yet watching you grow, whichever way nourished, your
body thriving on love more than method, slowly
unravels the knot of misconception— that motherhood's
success is measured in milk.
Gradually, I forge peace with my body's limits, learning
to honor what it could and couldn't do, finding new
paths to bonding and nurturing, releasing the
stranglehold of "should."
For those navigating similar waters, caught between
ideals and realities, between judgment and necessity:
Your worth as mother never flowed from your breasts.

21. After Loss

For those who've walked the lonely path of pregnancy loss, whose arms remain empty after hearts were full of hope.

She stands in the doorway of the nursery, yellow walls bright with unwarranted hope, crib assembled but never warmed, mobile spinning for absent eyes.

They use gentle euphemisms with her— "fetal demise," "no longer viable," "spontaneous termination," clinical terms for her catastrophic collapse.

She entered the hospital pregnant and left with empty arms, the physical weight of expectation replaced by grief's invisible heaviness.

Her body, betrayer and bereaved, continues producing milk for no one, breasts engorged with nourishment for a child who will never feed.

Well-meaning voices offer misguided comfort: "She can try again." "It wasn't meant to be." "At least she knows she can get pregnant."

As if her baby were replaceable, as if this child was not already beloved, named, imagined, already woven into the fabric of her future.

The physical reminders arrive without warning— the pregnant woman in the grocery store, the baby announcement on social media, the formula samples that still come by mail.

Her medical chart now bears the cruel tally: G1P0 – one pregnancy, zero living children, a mathematical equation that fails to capture the magnitude of her absence.

The grief counselor speaks of disenfranchisement, how her perinatal loss exists in shadow realm, too often minimized or quickly dismissed, lacking ritual or recognized mourning period.

Friends grow uncomfortable with her sadness, expecting recovery on arbitrary timeline, unaware that certain losses rewrite her soul, alter her internal landscape permanently.

She finds community in online support groups, in stories shared by others who understand the weight of tiny ashes in urns, the devastation of returning unused onesies.

Her partner grieves differently— through projects and plans and distraction, their pain dividing rather than uniting them, loss threatening to multiply in its wake.

Sleep brings her fleeting reunion in dreams where her baby remains safe within her, only to reawaken to fresh grief each morning, the loss experienced anew with consciousness.

She marks the due date on the calendar, a private
remembrance of what should have been, her baby's
birthday now an absence to acknowledge rather than a
presence to celebrate.

The question "Do you have children?" becomes a
minefield of social navigation— the honest answer too
heavy for casual conversation, the simplified "no" a
betrayal of her child's existence.

In time, her grief transforms rather than diminishes,
becoming less a drowning wave and more a permanent
alteration of landscape, a sacred scar she carries within.

Those who've walked this path before her say with
gentle understanding that eventual healing doesn't mean
forgetting or "moving on" but learning to live alongside
the absence.

For her child was real, was loved, existed— however
briefly, however silently— the imprint on her heart no
less significant for the shortness of their stay.

She releases lanterns on remembrance day, her baby's
name written among the stars, honoring the child she
carried but never held, the love that remains though they
are gone.

22. Maternal Metamorphosis

I catch my reflection in the window glass— a woman I'm still learning to recognize, transformed not just in body but in essence, metamorphosed by the journey of creation.

Who was I before this passage began? Sometimes I strain to remember clearly, that woman with her certainties and plans, her singular identity, her simpler heart.

The map of my body tells new stories— stretch marks silvered like lightning strikes, cesarean scar a permanent horizon line, breasts that have known both purpose and pain.

But the deeper changes lie beneath the surface— neural pathways rewired by sleepless nights, heart chambers expanded beyond previous capacity, boundaries between self and other forever blurred.

I've been broken open and reassembled, not carelessly but differently, the pieces fitting together in new arrangement, creating someone both familiar and strange.

They say motherhood changes you, but they rarely speak

of the death involved, the necessary surrender of former
self, the grieving that accompanies transformation.
In gaining a child, I lost a version of me, the woman who
moved freely through the world, unburdened by the
exquisite vulnerability of having her heart beating
outside her body.
Yet what emerged from pregnancy's crucible, from
labor's intensity, from postpartum's depths, is not
diminishment but expansion— the painful growth of
becoming more fully human.
I have descended into dark waters of doubt, faced fears I
never knew could exist, survived on less sleep than
seemed possible, discovered reservoirs of patience
previously untapped.
My boundaries now extend beyond my skin,
encompassing this small life connected to mine, yet
paradoxically, I've learned to draw firmer lines around
what matters, what deserves my energy.
Time has compressed and expanded simultaneously—
days that stretch like endless deserts, yet months that
vanish in heartbeats, the strange elasticity of maternal
chronology.
The woman I was hasn't disappeared entirely. Sometimes
I glimpse her in unexpected moments— in bursts of
laughter with old friends, in professional conversations
that engage my mind.
But she exists now within a larger context, her priorities

shifted, her vision widened, her understanding of love and fear deepened, her capacity for both joy and sorrow magnified.

This metamorphosis, painful as it sometimes was, has revealed strengths I never knew I possessed, vulnerabilities I needed to acknowledge, connections to generations of women before me.

For in becoming mother, I joined the ancient lineage of women transformed by creation's journey, each carrying forward the primal knowledge: that to bring forth life is to be forever changed.

I stand at the mirror and meet my new gaze— eyes that have witnessed beginning and ending, hands that have cradled both grief and wonder, heart that has broken and mended and grown.

This maternal metamorphosis continues still, with each milestone, each challenge, each year, not a single transformation but an ongoing becoming, a journey without destination but with profound purpose.